POCKET IMAGES

Around St Agnes

St Agnes Wesleyan Sunday School Tea at Peterville c. 1914.

POCKET IMAGES

Around St Agnes

Clive Benney

NONSUCH

Fish Seller at Churchtown, St Agnes c. 1904.

First published 1996
This new pocket edition 2006
Images unchanged from first edition

Nonsuch Publishing Limited
The Mill, Brimscombe Port,
Stroud, Gloucestershire, GL5 2QG
www.nonsuch-publishing.com

Nonsuch Publishing is an imprint of Tempus Publishing Group

British Library Cataloguing in Publication Data.
A catalogue record for this book is available from the British Library.

ISBN 1-84588-320-9

Typesetting and origination by Nonsuch Publishing Limited
Printed in Great Britain by Oaklands Book Services Limited

Contents

Acknowledgements   6

Introduction   7

1.   St Agnes Village   9

2.   Down Quay   25

3.   Villages to the South   45

4.   Villages to the North   63

5.   Groups and Events   77

6.   The Railway   89

7.   Mining   95

8.   Churches and Chapels, Tea Treats and Outings   107

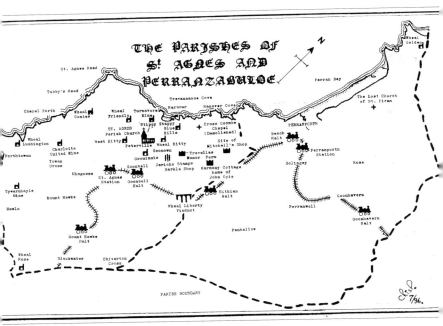

Acknowledgements

This book has given me a great deal of pleasure to research and compile. Everyone has been so helpful in many ways. I have been invited into people's homes to share their memories. Some have loaned me family photographs. I would like to thank all these people for their kindness: Roger Wonnacott, Roger Lacy, John Murrish, George Mitchell, Bill Morrison, Roger Radcliffe, Douglas Mitchell, Mrs Ruth Jennings, Mrs Freda Male, Frank Carpenter, John Sawle, Mrs Cathleen Nicholls, Mrs Vida Collins, Mrs Phyllis Thomas, George Williams, Mrs Peggy Libby and Kath Miles. I would also like to say thank you to Paddy Bradley for his advice in the compilation of this book, Chris Pearce for drawing the map, John Wotton for his photographic skills in making faded, unusable views into clear black and white copies, Jan Ball for her typing skills and her patience with the many changes I made to the original text, Terry Knight and the local studies department at Redruth and finally the Royal Institute of Cornwall, Truro for access to their old newspapers and photographs, some of which have been reproduced in this book.

Introduction

I have collected old photographs and postcards of the St Agnes area for twenty-one years and still feel the same excitement today when I find that previously 'unseen view'. A lot of people, like me, have an insatiable curiosity to peep into the past and see the villages and people as they used to be. Photographs help us to do this. As far back as 1839 photographs were taken in Cornwall and by the 1850s and '60s, there were numerous amateur and professional photographers operating in Cornwall. Several photographs in this book were taken in the 1890s and earlier, but the majority were taken between 1902 and 1920 and have postcard backs. The year 1902 was the start of postcard fever, and postcards could be bought for 1d or less and sent for $\frac{1}{2}$d in this country; everyone wrote, sent or collected them. Everything was photographed from street views to fires, accidents and celebrations; they were a way of sending pictorial news before the mass media of today. St Agnes at this time did not have its own photographer so the postcard demand was filled by photographers outside the area such as Mr E.A. Bragg from Illogan and Mr E. Argall from Truro. Many of their photographs appear in this book. In 1906 a Trevellas man called Samuel (Sammy) Solway, (who was employed at Wheal Kitty mine), needed something to supplement his income and recognised the growing hobby of postcard collecting and the need to record local events. He started in a small way using the spence (cupboard) under the stairs as his dark room. The venture was obviously successful as he continued for the next six years, and some of his finest cards are in my collection and about forty five are used in this book.

Many of you, no doubt, would like to climb into a time machine and go back through the years, I hope that in some small way this book enables you to do this.

Mithian, St Agnes, c.1905.

References

Royal Cornwall Gazette, 1900-20
St Agnes Museum Trust Journals, Nos 1 to 11
Perranporth, by Capt. W. Roberts
Story of a Village Street, by Frank Carpenter
Minutes of St Agnes Board of Highways, 1841-63

One

St Agnes Village

St Agnes from the Beacon c. 1908, showing the area around Churchtown. This is the oldest part of the village having grown up around the Parish church. Some of the white washed cottages at 'back of town' are believed to date from the sixteenth century. The two engine houses to the left of the view are part of West Kitty mine. Today the fields in the foreground are the sites of the new school and the houses and gardens of Beaconsfield Place and Trelawney Road. Despite the large amount of new building that has taken place over the last ninety years, St Agnes has managed to maintain its Cornish character and can claim with a great deal of truth to be one of the unspoilt villages of Cornwall.

Two women holding pitchers pose for the photographer beside the three thatched cottages in Goonvrea Road c. 1907. Today only the top cottage remains together with the tiled roof structure adjoining the middle cottage which has now been extended to make a house. The other two thatched cottages were destroyed by fire.

A sunny day in St Agnes c. 1907 as a wagon makes its way up Vicarage Road. The banner on the front tells us it belonged to Edward Brothers, millers and general merchants from Perranarworthal near Truro. The load being carried, probably flour, must have been very heavy because a 'chain horse' is being used to assist the horse between the shafts.

Vicarage Road c. 1905. The thatched building in the centre of the picture was a pork butchers owned by Mr Fred James. On the 23 October 1908 Mr James was woken at 1.30 a.m. to find his house full of smoke and the roof alight. The neighbours, together with PC Benney, tried unsuccessfully to save the furniture. The fire reached pails of lard and burnt fiercely. The house and stock were completely burnt and by morning only crumbling bare walls remained.

Vicarage Road c. 1925. Mr Hawke, a photographer from Helston, took this photo leaving his car AF 5929 in view at the roadside. Mr James' pork butchers has been replaced by a two storey building. The shop on the right belonged to Sidney Herbert Richards who was a photographic dealer, tobacconist, stationer and newsagent. On the left is Arthur Reynold's grocers shop.

Left: Tom Benney and Tom Stephens in 1905. Tom Benney, in the white jacket, was the town crier, bill poster and had a shop at Churchtown. Here he is putting a poster on the wall of the mortuary, now the lychgate, opposite the Railway Inn. Tom Stephens, holding the bucket, sold sand to housewives to put on their kitchen floors. This picture is slightly different to the usual one showing these two men; instead of seeing the poster on the right advertising a band performance at Redruth, the photograph has been cut to show the village blacksmith to the left. The blacksmith was situated where the 'Handyman' shop is today.

Below: The village blacksmith mentioned above and this photograph were taken the same day in 1905. The blacksmith was a very busy man at this time and absolutely indispensable. The community could not have survived without him. Horses could not work unless he shod them and he had to make and mend practically any implement the farmer needed.

Vicarage Road at the top of Rosemundy Hill c. 1904, showing a horse bus that travelled from St Agnes to Truro and Redruth. The journey to Truro took about an hour and a half. The two cottages in the centre of the picture were numbers 15 and 16 Vicarage Road which were knocked down in the late 1950s to make way for Trelawney Road.

Hooper and Son Baker's delivery wagon in Rosemundy Hill around 1906. The writing on the side describes the company as a high class confectioner. James Hooper had the bakery in Churchtown between 1906 and 1910.

Fore Street c. 1906. On the left is the Miners and Mechanics Institute. In 1891 Dr William Whitworth wrote to Passmore Edwards seeking help to provide a Miners and Mechanics Institute. Mr Edwards replied that he wanted to do something for the Parish of his birth and would be more than pleased to supply a building. He laid the foundation stone on the 7 June 1893.

Fore Street c. 1906 looking towards Churchtown with West Kitty engine house on the skyline. The road through the village at this time was often very dry and dusty and a nuisance to people living on the roadside. In July 1913 the road from Penwinnick to Churchtown was sprayed with tar. The shop in the bottom right hand corner of the photograph is a grocers owned by Richard Herbert Trenerry.

Fore Street to the Post Office around the end of the nineteenth and the beginning of the twentieth centuries. Note the stand pipe and the street lighting. Ten oil lamps at various sites in the village were introduced in 1890 and a lamplighter employed to light them 110 nights a year. The thatched building to the left of the picture with a flag over it was destroyed by fire in the 1930s when it was a fish and chip shop. The public toilets were built on the site.

St Agnes Post Office c. 1912. The Post Office moved here in 1903 having previously been at Churchtown where 'Needles-n-Pins' is today. The milk delivery wagon stands outside number 23 Churchtown which at this time was a sweet shop owned by Miss Sarah Rowe. Today there is no sign of the shop, the building having changed to a dwelling.

Churchtown around 1850. A very early photograph taken by Edward Opie of St Agnes. The original has been donated to St Agnes Museum Trust. This is possibly the oldest existing photograph of St Agnes showing the whole of Churchtown paved. On the 8 January 1852 at a meeting of the board of highways it was resolved that the pitch paving in Churchtown be taken up and the street be Mac Adamized and a neat curb of stones laid on each side.

Churchtown Market House c. 1890. It was built on a piece of wasteland around 1840 and extended across the top of the church from Bank House to the top of Town Hill. It was purchased in 1894 by the Vicar and Churchwarden for £250 and was demolished to allow better access to the church and for road widening.

A busy day at Churchtown c. 1905. Everyone stands very still for the photographer. The St Agnes Hotel was called Paulls Hotel with Henry Leigh the licensee. The left hand side of the hotel, which is now the public bar, was Treleaven and Co. Outfitters and Tailors. The Mac Adamized road through the pitch paving is clearly visible.

Churchtown c. 1912 when Matthew Pope Radcliffe had Churchtown Stores as a grocer, draper and general household merchant. The shop on the right sold most things from Cadburys chocolate, cocoa, tea at 1s 6d and Sunlight Soap. It also had a window full of postcards. The caravan in the centre of the view has 'God is love' on the end and is believed to be from the 'Church Army'.

An early postcard published c. 1908 by O.F. Stengel and Co. from London. On the right is the Capital and Counties Bank, hence the building's present name 'Bank House'. The present church was built in 1848 on the site of a fifteenth century church, the tower being the only part remaining of the old church. Note the iron railings on the church wall. To the left of centre is the St Agnes restaurant, grocer, draper and confectioner with the bakery to the right; both premises owned by James Hooper and Son.

Right: Postman Johnnie Cole delivers a letter to Tom Benney c. 1906. Tom lived in a cottage near the Porthvean Hotel then the White Hart. The boy playing the penny whistle is Harold Quick, born in 1902 who later went to America. Tom Benney had a shop close to where he lived at No. 9 Churchtown, next to the barbers shown in the picture below.

Below: Top of Town Hill back to Churchtown c. 1910. In the centre of the picture is No. 9 with a barber's pole outside. The shop on the right is a grocer and draper.

THE TOWN, ST. AGNES.

Ste Harris and his horse drawn butcher's wagon makes his way up through Goonown c. 1906. The young boy in the bottom right hand corner isn't going to stop eating his pasty just because his photograph is being taken!

Goonown Village c. 1905. A young boy with his dog, unaware of the changes that would take place in his life in the following years. Many young men left to find work in America. The Royal Cornwall Gazette newspaper of the 18 May 1909 reported: 'The drain of young St Agnes men to America continues, seven left on Friday and ten more next Friday. At this rate there will soon be a shortage of labour.'

Thomas John Delbridge had the bakery in St Agnes when this picture was taken c. 1910. He describes himself as a 'scientific baker', unlike his predecessor at the bakery James Hooper, who called himself a 'high class baker'. The youth stands with his horse drawn baker's wagon at Goonbell where Tresleigh Farmhouse is today.

Women and children across the road at Goonbell c. 1906, with Goonbell chapel in the distance behind them. The little primitive Methodist chapel was built halfway through the nineteenth century and remained a chapel until 1983 when it was converted into a dwelling. To the right of the chapel on the bend is a barn and the small white washed building next to it is believed to be the toilets for the cottages on the other side of the road.

Postmarked 7 July 1904, this postcard of Peterville shows the large open area that made it an ideal location for travelling shows. On the left at the bottom of Town Hill is a blacksmith. During the last century it was known as Dirtypool Forge with a blacksmith called Richard Stephens, alias 'Gunner Dick'. He loved company and had a large bench around his forge that would seat ten or twelve men all telling stories and jokes in the warmth.

A crowd parade through Peterville c. 1908. At the time this photograph was taken the wall on the right, at the bottom of British Road, contained a coal yard. The building inside the wall was built in 1779 and 1780 as a Dissenters' Meeting House or Preaching House as John Wesley preferred to call them. The shop on the opposite side of the road was a draper and grocer owned by Mr Letcher.

The rear view of four thatched cottages in Water Lane, St Agnes, destroyed by fire on 14 May 1909. The cause of the fire is unknown but after the alarm was raised a great effort was made to save the building with many people on the roof tearing at the thatch. The roof however went up in flames and nothing could be done to save the building. Truro Fire Brigade eventually arrived, but too late to prevent four families from being made homeless.

Front view of the above cottages. The remains of these four cottages can still be seen at the Peterville end of Waterlane. Behind on the skyline is Gooninnis engine house and headgear. The mine opened in an attempt to find tin on the extensions of the Wheal Kitty lode but the venture was unproductive. The engine house contained a 50 inch Cornish beam engine that had previously worked at Trevaunance and Penhalls mines. In 1910 the engine was moved to Goonvean clay works near Nanpean.

General view, St Agnes from the Perranporth Road c. 1906. A very busy road at this time with tons of tin ore from Wheal Friendly and West Kitty mines being conveyed by horse and cart to the stamps and processing plant at Jericho Valley. On the right is the headgear of Wheal Vottle. The two horses on the left are pulling a timber carrier. The rear two wheels and axle were adjustable forwards and backwards to accommodate the varying lengths of wood.

QUAY VALLEY & PETERVILLE ST AGNES.

Quay Valley towards Peterville c. 1910 with the derelict brass and iron foundry in the centre of the picture. When working, the foundry derived its power from a water wheel on the side of the building. A leat took water from the stream around the back and onto the wheel. The castle like building to the right on the skyline was built as a games room by Mr Coulter Hancock who owned Coulterville, now the Cleaderscroft Hotel.

Two

Down Quay

The valley running from Peterville to the beach at Trevaunance Cove was, for many centuries, the busiest valley in the area. The flow of water in the river from Peterville down the valley was powerful enough to run many water wheels that powered machinery and stamps. This postcard postmarked 29 December 1906 shows boys playing amongst the stones on the valley side.

Postmarked 2 July 1903 this postcard shows Quay Road on a bright and sunny day. The weather had obviously been nice for some time as the writer on the card says, 'Sorry I have not been able to send the cream but it is very scarce down here owing to the hot weather.' Behind the large house in the foreground, during the nineteenth century, there was a fish cellar where pilchards were salted and pressed.

The Golden Lion Pub c. 1890 when Edward Repper was the licensee. It was situated in the row of cottages shown in the view above. The pub was mostly used by miners working in the valley and at Wheal Kitty mine, who would walk down the valley side to the pub when their core (shift) had finished. Today the building is almost unrecognisable with many changes to the doors and windows.

A very rare view of Trevaunance Valley c. 1880 with many interesting points to look at. To the left on the hillside, Wheal Friendly engine house has not yet been built and just a horse whim is on the site. There is however quite a pile of mine waste to suggest the mine had been working for a time. On the far right on the skyline is Turnavore engine house and to its left, further back towards the Beacon, are the two engine houses and headgear of Trevaunance mine. This mine worked between 1843 and 1887. In the bottom right hand corner at the top of the beach, where the boat pen is today, there is a round buddle were tin sand was washed to remove impurities. The large building in the centre is a store for ropes, chains, wire, etc., owned by Mr Hitchens of the Trevaunance Pier Company who later sold the store and land around it to Mr W.J. Kemp, an old St Agnes boy living at Truro. In about 1920 the store was converted into flats by a local builder Eddie Tredinnick.

Trevaunance Valley c. 1906. The building on the right, now the Driftwood Spars Hotel, was a marine store and had previously been a fish cellar. During the 1920s the building fell into disuse and became semi derelict. In the early 1930s it was converted into the Driftwood Spars Hotel. The round building with the chimney in the centre of the picture is a kiln for firing bricks and called a 'bottle kiln' because of its shape.

A similar view to the one above but taken about twenty years later in the 1920s. Mr W.J. Kemp (mentioned on the previous page) had bought the land and buildings. Not only had he converted the building in the centre of the picture into flats but he had built Kemp's public tennis court and Kemp's store and tea-rooms on the corner overlooking the courts. Teas and ice-creams were served on the roof garden where people could watch the tennis or the sea.

Taken in 1903, this photograph shows the hive of activity that took place at Trevaunance Cove at this time. The harbour was in use and the area above the beach was a tin dressing plant. The large building is believed to have been at one time an iron foundry. A large pool of water stands where the beach car park is today and this water was used for the tin washing process.

By 1925, when this photograph was taken, many changes had taken place. The harbour had fallen down and because of the decline in mining, the tin dressing plant had disappeared and two bungalows built on the site. The old iron foundry building still remains with the left hand end being used as a dwelling. Tourism had reached St Agnes and the beach shelter had been built on the cliff above the beach.

Some early photographers with their cameras in 1910 stand and watch men paint their boats at the top of the beach. In front of the boat in the corner is the main adit of Polberro mine. This adit or tunnel dropped from the mine on the top of the cliff, draining water from the mine by gravity.

The Beach Tea House c. 1905, with what appears to be a Wesleyan choir outing sitting outside in the sun. By this time going to the beach was getting more and more popular. A newspaper of the day reported: 'Each succeeding bank holiday seems to secure a larger share of the public. It fully deserves it, as there is no safer beach on the North Coast of Cornwall.'

Trevaunance Cove 1910, looking up the valley from the beach with Wheal Friendly mine on the skyline. Two large water wheels are visible in the centre of the picture at the top of the beach, one of which is where the steps today go up to the beach shelter. In the centre of the beach a photographer has his camera and tripod set up, presumably taking a picture of the harbour.

A group of seine fishermen by one of their boats c. 1890. During the nineteenth century there were four seine companies at St Agnes and the same number at Perranporth. Huers were employed to walk the cliffs to watch for the shoals of pilchards. When spotted the cry 'Hevva Hevva' was called and instantly the beach came alive with seiners putting their boats to sea.

St Agnes Harbour c. 1900. Many attempts were made to build a harbour at Trevaunance Cove. The first in 1632, was never completed, being destroyed by the winter gales. The second in 1684 at Old Quay, nearer the Point than the first attempt. Several hundred pounds was spent cutting down the cliff to make a new entrance (between Man Rock and the cliff) and buoying up great rocks to close the old entrance to the cove. The winter gales however, knocked down in hours, what had taken several months to build. The third in 1699 was designed by Winstanly of Eddystone Lighthouse fame. This was a much more professional undertaking. The quay was completed and looked very strong and substantial butting against the Western Cliffs. Sea traffic continued for the next six years and a fishery was established, but unfortunately in August 1705 a storm again destroyed the quay. In 1709 another quay was built on the same site with a similar construction technique to Winstanly's. This quay lasted twenty years, but in 1730 was completely destroyed. In 1793 an Act of Parliament was passed for: 'Erecting and making a pier and harbour in the cove of Trevaunance in the Parish of St Agnes.' The work had to be completed within seven years from the date of the Act of Parliament. Work began immediately. The outer walls were made from large dressed granite blocks drilled through from top to bottom and laid so they overlapped, allowing iron bars to be driven through the holes locking the blocks together. An inner wall was then built and the cavity between the walls filled with rubble and mortar made from stone and lime. The quay surface was then paved.

A sailing ship enters the harbour c. 1905. Entering the harbour during the winter gales, even at high tide, was totally impossible and there would have been periods of days or weeks with no shipping movement in or out. Even on a calm day sailing unaided directly into the harbour was hazardous and many ships, as in this picture used a 'hobbling' boat to guide or tow them into the harbour.

The confines of the harbour meant that once in, it was almost impossible to turn the vessel around, therefore they had to leave backwards, stern first. Having cleared the harbour entrance they had to quickly turn starboard and head out to sea. Above, a ship carries out this manoeuvre c. 1900.

Once in the harbour the ships moored under the cliff as here c. 1900. From this position the ship was unloaded using boxes or kibbles hauled onto one of the three wooden gantries on top of the cliff. As the full box went up the empty box lowered, and at rest both boxes would come to a mid point part way down the cliff.

A wooden gantry above the harbour c. 1900. The rough timbers fitted into the cliff and supported the platform. One wonders how this could have supported the tons of coal and other goods hauled up the cliff face over the years. There were two main gantries, like the one above, and a third smaller one in front of what is now Gull Cottage. The cable, from the boxes, passed over the pulley wheel to the horse whim further back on the cliff top.

A horse whim above the harbour c. 1890. The cable went around the large drum and back to a second wheel on the gantry and down to a second box. The two horses would walk in a circle rotating the drum and therefore raising and lowering the boxes.

Two ships in the harbour c. 1890. At low tide boats in the harbour were left high and dry on the sandy bottom. This also restricted its use. Even with a calm sea the entrance lay virtually on the mean low water mark which made it impossible to operate with any sizeable shipping below half tide. The man standing on the sand between the boats gives you an idea of the size of the ships entering the harbour.

Having unloaded their cargo the ships moved across the harbour to the North Quay for loading with tin ore, copper ore or ballast, as here, c. 1900.

A ship moored against the North Quay c. 1890. Tin or copper ore or ballast was sent from the cliff top down a chute and onto the little wooden trolley on rails and then along the harbour wall to be loaded.

Left: The Cornish Lass moored against the North Quay in the 1890s. On the 6 January 1896 the 60 ton ketch left St Agnes harbour carrying ballast, part of which was made up of plate punchings, having previously discharged coal from Lydney. The wind was from the west and not very strong. She cleared the harbour entrance and had reached Trevaunance Point when the wind died away, whereupon the tide and ground sea carried her across the cove towards Trevellas.

Below: Once she was between Trevaunance and Trevellas she was wrecked on the Maddock Rocks. The unfortunate vessel never got off and soon broke up, becoming a total loss.

A highlight of the year in St Agnes was the annual Regatta. Practically the whole populace flocked down to the harbour to watch the sports and sailing events. The event was revived in 1906 after many years without it. Saturday 1 September 1906 was the day and thousands watched the events from the harbour, beach and cliffs. The weather and sea conditions were ideal.

Walking the greasy pole event 1906 with the pole out over the harbour entrance. Everyone failed to walk along the pole until permission was given to wear shoes. W. Matthews of Newquay won the event. During the events Perranporth Volunteer Band played a selection of music.

Other Regatta events were the boat races. There were three classes for sailing boats depending on length, and a rowing and sculling race. This picture c. 1908 shows sailing boats after the race inside the harbour against the North Quay. Hundreds of people in their Sunday best are watching the races from the harbour wall.

The first prize winner in the Sailing Boat Race, in the harbour under the cliff c. 1908. Another water event was swimming races open to all-comers, men, under 18's and under 14's. Note to the left the smaller South Quay was not attached to the cliff face. The ladder provided the only access from the cliff onto this quay at high water.

An event arranged primarily for the enjoyment of miners was the drilling contest. The object of the competition was for teams of two or three men to hand drill into a piece of granite for fifteen minutes, the winners being the team that drilled the deepest hole. The winners of the above competition in 1910 were E. Sandercock and R. Hall who drilled a depth of $22\frac{1}{16}$ inches.

Here we see the men who competed in the 1912 rock drilling competition. The winners were E. Sandercock and W.J. Sandow $24\frac{1}{2}$ inches, second R. Trezise and F. Barkle 23 inches and third H. Morcom and W. Harris $21\frac{5}{8}$ inches. The prizes for the event were given by the management of West Kitty mine and the judges were Captain J. Chenoweth, C. Prisk and Mr Doble.

The boat *The Harriet* in the harbour, c. 1908, under the North Quay at low tide. This picture gives some idea of the height and structure of the harbour wall. *The Harriet* with its owner Mr Rowles competed regularly in the regatta races and in 1908 won the 1st Class boat race in a time of 3 hours 13 minutes. Close behind in second place was *GIPP* with Mr Repper in 3 hours 16 minutes, and third *ASB* with Mr Sawle in 3 hours 18 minutes.

By the time this picture was taken in c. 1914 the harbour had become deserted and the unloading gantries taken away. It comes as no surprise when, on the 15 July 1915, a stone was washed out of the outer wall, no-one bothered to replace it. Later that year in an October storm the breach in the wall was made so large that a horse and cart could be driven into it. History was repeating itself and the following year the North Quay was practically demolished. The south wall soon followed.

Above: Between 1873 and 1877 four schooners were built on St Agnes Beach. The first launched on the 20 January 1873 was named *St Agnes*. The second, pictured above being built, was the *Goonlaze* launched on the 3 July 1874. The third, the *Trevellas* was launched on the 21 June 1876.

Right: The fourth and last schooner to be built on St Agnes Beach was the *Lady Agnes*, pictured here under the cliff in St Agnes harbour, unloading her cargo, c. 1895. She was a two masted schooner of 91 tons, launched on 6 September 1877 and registered at Hayle. She was sold many times during her life, the last being on the 4 November 1941 to Walter White of Croydon but she never went to sea again. She was eventually broken up in 1948 having lain derelict through the Second World War.

Trevaunance Valley c. 1905, from the top of Rocky Lane towards the beach. The old thatched cob cottages are beginning to get into a bad state of repair, especially the thatch and by 1920 the cottages were roofless and derelict. Today their site and the area in the foreground is the Little Orchard Village.

Bicycles propped up on the roadside at the bottom of Rocky Lane c. 1910. Two young men pose for the photographer, who presumably owns the third bike, with his camera case beside it. The foreground has changed considerably over the years, the cliffs in the distance appeared to have changed very little.

Three

Villages to the South

Moyle's blacksmith shop c. 1906, situated on the cross roads at Chiverton near the Chiverton Arms Public House. The blacksmith at Chiverton was a very busy man, not only did he have local work but also passing trade on the Turnpike road that ran from Truro to St Agnes. Between 1750 and 1820 Turnpike roads were introduced because of the increase in mining and road transport. Trustees obtained an Act of Parliament naming roads to be improved enabling them to raise money. Roads were measured, repaired and milestones set up. Trustees had the right to charge tolls. The Turnpike road from Chiverton to St Agnes had a toll house and gate at the six milestone near the entrance to the Teagle's factory. Charges were made according to the number of animals pulling wagons or animals driven. Turnpike roads in Cornwall ceased in 1874 after 120 years because of the railways coming to Cornwall. On the 19 December 1874 the Toll House, Toll Board Gate and granite and wood posts at the six milestone were sold.

Blackwater Hill c. 1910, with two horses pulling a wagon slowly down the hill into Blackwater. The parish boundary between St Agnes and Kenwyn goes up the left hand side of the hill making the hill in Kenwyn Parish. During the 1850s numerous disputes took place between the two parishes as to which should carry out the repairs to the road surface.

Blackwater c. 1905, when the main road went through what is now the lay-by. On the right where the haywagon stands, is the site of the first weigh-bridge. It weighed loads of up to five tons and had an eight foot top plate. Animals, hay, straw and any farm produce was weighed here. In the mid 1930s a twenty ton weigh-bridge was installed and in the mid 1950s the present forty ton. On the left behind the monkey puzzle tree was the post office, grocer and draper. William Hooper was the sub postmaster.

Blackwater Reed and Brass Band c. 1906. In 1900 the village had a fife and drum band that practised in a stable near Blackwater chapel. In 1902 the Brass Band was formed under the leadership of Corporal C. Retallack DCLI. Bandsmen met in a hut near the railway line for practice.

Blackwater Wesleyan chapel 1905. Built in 1822; this date appears in stone above the door. When built it was a very plain building, the floor was earth and the seats were forms without backs or ends. Men sat on one side and ladies the other. Light was from tallow candles, the same as miners used. The village policeman stands beside his bicycle on this postcard postmarked 1 December 1905 which was sent to Transvaal, South Africa.

An Argall postcard entitled 'Blackwater showing Institute' c. 1903. Blackwater's most famous son was John Passmore Edwards, born at Blackwater on the 24 March 1823. After starting life in a humble home he eventually moved from Cornwall to become a city journalist and lecturer, newspaper editor and member of Parliament for Salisbury. In 1889 the Vicar of Mithian appealed to Mr Edwards for a few books for a small club in the village. He replied that he would send 500 volumes and if the land could be found, he would build a new institute. The land was of course found.

The opening of Blackwater Institute in 1890 which John Passmore Edwards attended. At the ceremony he said, 'Nothing has given me more pleasure than to give this to my native village and within a hundred yards of my old home.' The village school was closed for the occasion to allow children to witness the ceremony.

The crossroads at Blackwater c. 1920. PC Stephens stands in the road near his police house in Coronation Terrace. The man on the right holding the pony is James Nicholls who made the tea at the various chapel tea treats. He had the nickname 'Jimmy Cuptea'!

The Red Lion Inn at Blackwater c. 1910. The horse and cart nearest the camera is believed to have belonged to Mrs Rowe who went around the area selling vegetables. The horse tucks into its nose bag while waiting for her to return.

Blackwater School Garden c. 1920. The garden was situated on the opposite side of the lane to the school where the small playing field is today. The card was sent to a Blackwater County Councillor by Mr A.J. Whale, headmaster of the school. Only the boys are gardening, no equality in those days!

The railway bridge at West End, Blackwater 1903. On the end of the house next to the bridge is Miss Lanyon's shop. Her view to Blackwater was totally blocked when the embankment to carry the Chacewater to Newquay branch line was built in 1902. Also cottages that stood on the other side of the road had to be demolished.

Wheal Rose Village c. 1910 and Wheal Rose engine house in the distance. This mine produced copper and a small amount of tin and worked between 1826 and 1872. The child in the road watches the photographer while sitting in his pedal car.

A broken down portable steam engine at Wheal Rose c. 1914, with what appears to be a broken stub axle. The portable engine was horse drawn to its working site. A well used piece of machinery during harvest time to power the threshing machine, and an accident like this would have been most unwelcome by the farmers.

Another accident at Wheal Rose c. 1918. This time a traction engine owned by Mr George Carlyon of Mount Hawke has ended up on its side. The traction engine weighed many tons and it would have been extremely difficult to right it again.

A horse drawn hearse at Skinners Bottom in January 1920. The crowds watch as a second comes onto the road. The deceased were a man and woman believed to have been murdered at their home. Robbery was at first thought to be the motive and detectives from Scotland Yard were called in to investigate. After a long enquiry they came to the conclusion they had killed each other as there was no evidence that anything had been stolen. However, the jury disagreed and returned the verdict of wilful murder by person or persons unknown.

The Valley from Echo Corner, Porthtowan to the Beach c. 1905. Echo Corner is devoid of buildings except for the remains of South Towan mine engine house and stack. Until 1934 the St Agnes Parish boundary followed the stream from Manor Parsley down this valley to the sea at Porthtowan. In 1934 the boundary from Mawla was straightened and now goes from Mawla to the junction with the old road leading across Nancekuke common (now RAF Portreath). It follows this road a short distance before turning right and over the cliff to the sea near Tobban Rock.

Old Cottages at Porthtowan c. 1905. On the right is the old corn mill which derived its power from the water wheel seen on the end. Today these cottages and mill are almost unrecognisable. The mill has been made into a two storey dwelling. The cottages now have gardens in front with hedges against the road.

Porthtowan c. 1900. The thatched building in the bottom right hand corner are the Old Coast Guards Houses. Tourism had obviously reached Porthtowan early as already there are tea houses and stabling for horses on the beach. In the centre of the picture in the small meadow there appears to be a tennis court marked on the grass.

Croust time at Porthtowan c. 1904. Two tin streamers stop to eat their pasties. These men made a living by washing beach sand for tin deposits that had been washed down the stream from the mines further up the valley.

A typical August Bank Holiday c. 1906. Large crowds made their way from Redruth and the surrounding area to Porthtowan. Besides the permanent tea rooms, enterprising traders have set up stalls on the beach selling food and sweets. Most people however brought their own picnics of pasties, saffron buns and heavy cake.

PORTHTOWAN NR REDRUTH. No 15.

Taken the same day as the above picture, this time from the West Cliff. In the bottom right hand corner are the stables, for the horses used for pulling the various modes of transport. They all appear to be full as many horses stand outside trying to find shade from the sun.

No horses out in the sun on this hot summer's day c. 1910. All types of horse drawn vehicles were used to get to the beach including jingles, traps and Jersey cars. On the right are the stables and nearer the sea the four tea rooms of Glasson's, Nicholl's, Rickard's and Gill's.

The Electric Company Excursion Brake to Porthtowan in the summer of 1904. The Electric Company ran brakes (a type of transport) from its terminus at Redruth on Wednesdays and Thursdays hoping to increase the popularity of the resort. They advertised: 'That not only would it be a pleasant ride to Porthtowan but those making the trip would be able to enjoy a half day romp on the sands.'

Glasson's tea room at Porthtowan c. 1908 with a shop at the rear. The man in the shirt sleeves and waistcoat is believed to be Mr Glasson standing beside the delivery man in the white coat. The delivery wagon to the left of the picture, is most probably from a local bakery.

Cross Coombe and Trevellas chapel outing to Porthtowan c. 1908, outside Nicholl's tea room. Above them on the roof is the figurehead from the *Rose of Devon* which was wrecked off Porthtowan in 1897.

A delivery wagon makes its way up through Mount Hawke village c. 1908, and it appears to be the same man that delivered to Glasson's tea rooms, Porthtowan on the previous page. Mount Hawke differs from most Cornish villages in that it has no early history of association with church or manor. It is a mining village of comparatively late origin like numerous other villages in the county, and has survived the decay of the mines.

The blacksmith shop, Mount Hawke c. 1905. Edgar Rodda was the blacksmith with Harold Wilkins his apprentice. The man on the left is Charlie Harris. Despite being blind he used to go to Redruth every Friday to collect newspapers for the village; he also collected and conveyed sand from St Agnes Beacon for housewives to sprinkle on their kitchen floors.

Children outside Uren's Drapers and Grocers shop, Mount Hawke c. 1910. Many early photographers liked children across the road, or had them in their photographs. This guaranteed sales to parents of the children, when they returned later to sell their postcards. On the right the wooden railings on the wall are outside the former Mount Hawke Post Office.

Further down Mount Hawke towards Banns, more children line up across the road for the photographer. The postcard is postmarked 24 December 1904 and sent as a Christmas card by Adeline to a Miss Hore at Exeter. The message reads: 'If you look at this card you will see Ethel Aver and I. We have coats on. I am now going up to Mount Hawke with cream for you. I wish you a Merry Christmas and Happy New Year.' On the right is Griggs grocery shop and the building further up the road to the left is Philip Jones' cobblers shop.

Philip Jones' cobblers shop, Mount Hawke c. 1905. Philip on the right was born at St Ives in 1865 and learnt his trade at Truro. Philip's son Will, aged 92 at the time of writing, was born at Mount Hawke in 1904, now living in America, provided much of the information about his father and Mount Hawke:

'Father told me that when he was learning his trade at Truro his mother would make him six pasties each week which he took to Truro and by the time he ate the last pasty the potato was very slippery! Father started his shop in Mount Hawke around 1886 because it was close to the tin mines. He made heavy hob nail boots for miners of St Agnes, St Day, Redruth and Camborne and also for local farmers. When World War One came they took all the men from the farms and almost all the horses. My dad had to make army boots. He had Will Pearce learning his trade with him which helped him. My dad's shop had seats in it and a stove, so it was always nice and warm, so people not working would come and sit in the shop. Several men came home from Mexico, India, Spain and Canada, who had all left Cornwall years before to work in the gold mines. They all told stories about being in these countries.'

Hand made working boots were expected to last at least two years of hard farm work. A new pair cost two weeks wages and they were therefore well looked after and repaired and patched many times before finally needing replacing.

Right: The Old Mill, Mount Hawke c. 1906.
A very busy place with all the local farmers
having their corn crushed here. The mill
was owned and run by Walter Plummer and
his mother (both seen in the picture). The
machinery was worked by a water wheel to the
left of the mill, and the water to turn the wheel
came from a mill pool at the bottom of Gover
Hill. The pool was dammed up at night and
released in the morning to run down a leat
behind the mill and to the water wheel.

Below: William May's grocer and drapers shop
at Towan Cross in 1904. William May is seen
pushing a heavy bag of flour on his sack trolley.
Beatrice May is riding the horse.

THE OLD MILL, MOUNT HAWKE.

Chapel Porth on a postcard postmarked 18 July 1913 and showing the old mine workings where the car park is today. The building in the centre of the view was built around 1905 by Joe Tremewan for his niece Winnie Rickard, who used it as a tea and boarding house. In July 1906 a lifebuoy was put on the side of the building, following a drowning in the bay. The lifebuoy was in a case with a glass front which had to be smashed in an emergency.

Higher Bal, St Agnes c. 1905. This little hamlet grew up in the highly productive Polberro mining area. There were many mines in the area, some with wonderful names such as Great Pratt, Dolga, Wheal Squidler and Seal Hole. The word Bal, as in Higher Bal, is the Cornish for mine. For many years Higher Bal had its own little Methodist chapel to serve the needs of the people in the Beacon area.

Four

Villages to the North

Mithian c. 1906. Situated about equal distance between St Agnes and Perranporth and is said to be one of the oldest villages in Cornwall. Many of the houses are three or four hundred years old and built of 'Cob' (a clay substance reinforced with straw and horse hair). Originally they would have had thatched roofs but now only a few remain. The white thatched building on the right is Mithian Post Office and the wooden building on the left is George Roger's cobblers shop.

Mithian c. 1914 looking up through the village towards Roger's shop and George Roger's new flat roofed cobblers shop on the end of the building. The white cottage in the centre of the view was destroyed by fire shortly after this photograph was taken. A new house was built on the site.

Children and young men line across the road c. 1908. The large building behind them in the centre of the photograph is the old Manor House. Now divided into cottages, it was once occupied by a French Nobleman and later the Wynslade family who, for their great revenues, were dignified with the title 'Esquire of the White Spurs'. The house on the right, with the name board over the door, is Mrs Edith Mabel Ennors' grocers shop.

Posted in June 1906, this postcard was sent by Mary who lived at Underwood, Mithian, a cottage on the left, down the hill. According to the writer: 'Cecil is looking out around the corner of the white washed wall.' A horse drawn delivery wagon stands outside the Miners Inn and the lady with the pitchers has either bought something from it or collected water from the well that was in the cellar of the inn.

More children across the road in 1906. Behind is the Miners Inn, now the Miners Arms, reputed to have been built in 1577 and this date appears on one of the decorative plaster ceilings. There is a secret stone lined passage that goes from the inn in the direction of the Manor House on the opposite side of the road. A villager who went down the tunnel many years ago said the centre portion had collapsed under the road.

Threshing corn at Mithian Farm in 1908. A portable steam engine works the threshing machine using a belt from the large fly wheel. The portable engine and the threshing machine would usually be owned by a contractor who pulled the machinery by horse from farm to farm during harvest time.

The same day as above and the bagged grain is ready to be taken away. Charlie Brokenshire stands beside the horse in the shafts. Another 'chain horse' is attached to the front to assist in pulling the great weight. Each bag of grain weighing over 1 cwt.

Right: The whole family are helping to make the hayrick at Sunberry Farm, Trevellas in 1911. After drying in the field the hay was carried by horse and cart to where the rick was to be built. The rick would have been round or oblong and on completion it would have been thatched with wheat straw.

Below: Randell Mitchell holding the bulls nose outside Trevellas Manor Farm c. 1910. To the rear of the bull is Russell Mitchell. The bull and the farm were owned by John Henry Mitchell, known locally as Ma's John.

Mithian School children c. 1905. The school was opened on the 13th July 1874 for 250 to 270 children and cost £888 to build. In May 1905 Mr E. Joad, a school's inspector visited the school and made the following remarks. 'The school is, in the main, well taught; written work is neat and composition is of more than average merit; but more variety of treatment is needed in the arithmetic of the lower standards.'

Mr Harry Sandow of White Street, Mithian, stands outside his house with his family the morning after a fire totally destroyed his home. During the night of the 30 August 1906 neighbours discovered the fire which had attacked the rear of the house and the thatched roof. They were able to save the furniture and the stairs. They also saved the door and windows and you can see where the walls have been chipped away around the windows to get them out.

Right: Alf Crebo's blacksmith shop at Barkla Shop c. 1900. Alf is here working at the anvil while his assistant pulls the handle to work the bellows for the forge. The bellows created a draught of air needed to bring the fire to a sufficient temperature to heat the iron for working. The blacksmith was situated where the house called Glen Carne is today. There has been a blacksmith at Barkla Shop for a long time. At the meeting of the Board of Highways on the 7 January 1847 it was announced that, 'Mr Woolcock is about to take down his old smiths shop at Barkla Shop and about to build a new one. Land would become available for road widening!' Mr Crebo was very busy around 1901 and 1902 with the building of the Chacewater to Perranporth railway and particularly with the building of Wheal Liberty viaduct just a short distance away up the valley. Horses transporting stone from local quarries needed regular shoeing.

Below: John Tredinnick's carpenters and wheelwright shop at Barkla Shop c. 1908, and situated next to the blacksmith (above). Many jobs the carpenter or wheelwright did needed the blacksmith to finish them off. During the making of wooden wheels, seen in the picture, the blacksmith added the iron to the hub and the iron tyre around the outside. The red hot iron tyre, when in place, was cooled quickly with water causing it to shrink and force the wooden joints tightly together.

On the 15 July 1909 there was a disastrous fire at Zion House, Trevellas. The house, consisting of eight rooms with a shop and store attached, was owned by Mr J.T. Mitchell, a general merchant and auctioneer. Around 1850 the building was used as a 'Meeting House', hence its name. In one of the floors of the dwelling house a part of the pulpit used by Billy Bray was also destroyed.

Mrs Menadue stands outside her shop at Trevellas c. 1906. Her husband and two sons are beside the wall. The shop was a draper and grocers and sold their own ginger beer in brown stoneware bottles, made in Staffordshire by Denby. The bottle had 'W.T. Menadue' stamped on the side. The shop later became Trevellas Post Office but today the shop front has disappeared, becoming part of the dwelling house.

Perranporth in the 1890s showing the valley from Perrancoombe to the bay. The cottages in the foreground with the white gable end have a lovely view down the valley to the beach and the road up through Perrancoombe just in front. This was to change with the coming of the railway in 1903 (see picture below). Before the building of the road out of Perranporth via Liskey Hill, this road through Perrancoombe was the main road to Truro.

About thirty years later c. 1925, we see the railway embankment built for the Chacewater to Perranporth railway. The white cottages have lost their view and look onto the embankment and are now in a dead end, the road diverted to the other side of the embankment from St Michael's church to Riverside. The first indication of the coming of the railway was the appearance of surveyors in the fields with their instruments. Soon the navvies invaded the village seeking lodgings.

A view across the Perrancoombe Valley towards the Convalescent Home c. 1893. The home looks new, having been built in 1892, a gift to the village of Perranporth by Passmore Edwards and dedicated in remembrance of his mother. The Home offered recuperation mainly for patients leaving the Royal Infirmary at Truro. The field in the foreground was the site of Perranporth's first tennis court in 1896.

An early view taken from a glass lantern slide showing boats under the Western Cliffs c. 1890. At high tide the boats were afloat and large ropes were used to moor them. The ropes varied in diameter depending on the size and weight of the boat, some were four inches in diameter.

The Bar, Perranporth c. 1890, with seine fishing boats high and dry on the sand. The building behind the boats is a fish cellar. This building later became Dick Mitchell's Enterprise Motors, reputed to be the first motor bus service to operate in Cornwall. In the distance is the engine house and stack of Wheal Leisure Mine.

The sea wall and promenade, Perranporth c. 1915. Built about 1910, the public take advantage of the wall to sit on. The inner beach in the distance was rarely covered by the tide and, as seen here, the sand slowly piled up in front of the nearby houses. Eventually the area was bought by the Parish Council. A retaining wall was built and the area grassed, giving an open area where children could play.

Wood Street c. 1908, from Tywanhayle Bridge to the Bar. As the name implies the buildings in this street were made of wood. The shop on the right is Harvey-Mitchell's Cycle and Motor repairs and next to it is Harvey-Mitchell's Universal Stores which, by the shop front, appears to sell everything. This street today is Beach Road.

A merry-go-round on the promenade at Perranporth c. 1905. Identification of the location made possible by the inclusion of the three storey building to the right, and the fish cellar to the left. Both these buildings are visible in the top photograph on the previous page.

Mr Govier, the photographer, stands on the railway embankment to take this photograph of Bolingey, c. 1908. Everyone stops to look up at him except the delivery man unloading his wagon on the left of the view. The white building he is delivering to is the old Bolingey Post Office, grocer and draper. This building has now gone and a large dwelling house built on its site.

Bolingey c. 1907, showing the Bolingey Hotel now the Bolingey Inn. The licensee at this time was S.J. Ball. Adjoining the hotel is a row of thatched roofed cottages, the one nearest the hotel has a sign on it, 'Offices, New Wheal Leisure Mining Company'.

The Lost Church Perranporth c. 1920. To preserve the ancient building from weathering and vandalism it was covered and enclosed by a concrete structure in 1910. As seen here it provided little space and lighting for the visitor. In 1980 as a result of flooding and vandalism the church and concrete structure were covered with an artificial hill, marked today with a plaque on the top, and a cross on top of a sand dune a few hundred yards away.

Some residents of Lower Rose stand in the muddy road c. 1906. The lady leaning on the garden wall by the white gate gets water for her cottage from a well just outside the front door. A bucket attached to a rope sits on top of the winder.

Five

Groups and Events

A parade makes its way down Town Hill into Peterville in 1904. Before the days of televisions, videos and computers, annual village events were well supported as were the choirs, bands and numerous sports teams.

Coronation Day Thursday 22 June 1911. In Cornwall every town and hamlet made a whole hearted effort to celebrate the event. At St Agnes rain fell for most of the morning until midday when there was a marked improvement. Here we see the start of the afternoon proceedings at 2 p.m. with the assembly of the children and others in the field at Penwinnick Road. Mr J. Angwin then led the singing of the Coronation Hymn 'Raise the song ye loyal voices, save the King, save the King'.

Following the singing, a procession was formed, to walk around the village in the following order: Gentlemen on horse back, Coastguards under Chief Officer Gordon, Boys Brigade under Capt. J. Eudey and Lieut. Rogers, St Agnes Band with Bandsmaster Robins, St Agnes College, Town and Mithian Council Schools, Members of Friendly Societies, General Public and Carriages. Here the men on horseback followed by Coastguards, are in Penwinnick Road by the cemetery gates.

This picture appeared in my first book and I asked for help in identifying the event. It is clear now this is part of the Coronation day procession. The Gentlemen on horseback have passed and here we have the Coastguards followed by the Boys Brigade. The parade is passing under a lovely floral arch at the top of British Road. On returning to the field, each child under 14 years was given a mug.

In the evening at 7 p.m. there was the Coronation Carnival Parade which took mainly the same route as the afternoon event. Here we have Miss A. Hicks, the first prize winner, in the ladies decorated bicycle class. J. Smith won the men's class.

The first prize winner in the Decorated Wagon class was Mrs S.J. Hooper and Miss Mitchell with entry 'Flower Girls', seen here. Other classes included Decorated Donkey Chaise won by F. James, Comic won by Sydney Williams and F. Harper with 'Home Sweet Home', and Fancy Dress won by Mrs Seal as a Welshwoman.

Butcher Bill Harris and his entry 'Haymaking' received second prize in the Trade class. He was beaten by Miss Tregea with her entry 'Dairy'. In third place was St Agnes Bakery. After the carnival a bonfire was lit on the Beacon. A block of oil for lighting the fire was given by Petro Patent Solid Oil Co. which was sent free with carriage paid.

The Juvenile Lodge of St Agnes Oddfellows at Churchtown on Saturday 13 August 1910 as part of their annual Fete. Taking part were 86 boys, 65 girls and several adults. They had previously assembled at the Oddfellows Hall (now the Meadery), and, headed by St Dennis band, paraded through the village.

After the above parade, sports, confined to lodge members, took place in a field in Penwinnick Road. Events included flat races for boys and girls, high jump and potato picking. Here the under 15 boys are ready for the start of the egg and spoon race. The policeman watches to make sure no-one uses their thumb. The race was won by H. Stribley, second was H. Radcliffe and third W. Thomas.

The harbour regatta and sports were held on Monday 7 August 1911. Various boat and swimming events took place together with many land events. Here is the start of the men's over 40, 100 yards race which was won by S.J. Hooper with J. Roberts second and Mr Dunstan third. The big man second from the right is butcher Bill Harris who didn't do very well in this event. He did however win the 28 lb weight putting event.

Hospital Sunday c. 1906. This was held every summer to raise money for the Royal Cornwall Infirmary and the District Nursing Association. Headed by Camborne Town Band under Bandmaster Mr Uren; the Rechobites, Philanthropic and Oddfellows paraded through the village with a collection on route. Here the parade has reached Peterville and the band has stopped to play for the crowd. In 1906 the parade collected £7 0s 8½d.

A picnic party at Trevellas Porth in 1908. Members of Cross Coombe Choir, family and friends made a trip every summer to Trevellas Beach or Loves Valley to have a picnic. A large white table-cloth was placed on the ground, seen to the left of the photograph, and everyone's food was laid on it. When the time came to eat, everyone helped themselves.

In 1909 the above group held their picnic at Loves Valley. This sheltered valley was on the cliff on the Perranporth side of Trevellas Porth and access to the valley was via the coastal path or lane at the rear of Cross Coombe Farm. The lane and the farm disappeared when Trevellas air field was built at the beginning of the Second World War.

St Agnes coastguards standing in front of their rocket apparatus at the coastguard station in 1904. The apparatus was used to rescue people from wrecked ships. A rocket with a line attached was fired from the cliff top onto the ship. Once the line was attached to the ship the crew were pulled along the rope to the cliff in a harness called a breeches buoy. Every three months the coastguards were drilled in the use of the apparatus. On 24 January 1906 the St Agnes brigade were drilled and the time taken was thirteen minutes. This was much longer than usual and the reason given was that several members occupied new positions. Formerly the brigade was considered the smartest on the coast when the drill only took six and a half minutes. On the 27 December 1900 the St Agnes brigade under Chief Officer Woods rushed to Perranporth to assist the Perranporth brigade when the French barque *La Seine* got into difficulties. After many attempts a line reached the barque and was secured. The French sailors on board did not understand the instructions and what to do. Eventually a boy came ashore who said there were twenty-four crew on board. These men were hauled ashore two at a time in the breeches buoy.

On Monday 8 June 1908, St Agnes was invaded by nearly 200 boys, members of several Cornish Boys Brigades. The gathering was to celebrate the permanent amalgamation of the St Agnes and Perranporth companies. After assembling at the Church Hall at 2 p.m. they marched to the football field at Football Lane for a march past. Here the boys march through Peterville led by Mr J. Eudey.

The opening of Trevellas Men's Institute on Saturday 6 December 1913 by Mr J. Hitchens. The foundation stone had been laid on 27 June 1912. After the opening there was a public tea and concert in Mithian School. In the evening West Kitty male voice choir gave a concert.

St Agnes Town Band c. 1907. The band was formed as a constituted town band in October 1907. Prior to this St Agnes had no town band and was served for its musical needs by one or two independent groups of musicians. The first band master was Mr John Paul and the band soon became well established and demands on the band were many. In 1911 ill health forced Mr Paul to resign and Mr Harry Robins of Perranporth succeeded him.

On Saturday 22 August 1908 St Agnes band held a sports day to raise money to pay off a debt on the large instruments of the newly formed band. Apart from a shower in the afternoon the weather was ideal and nearly a thousand people paid for admission. Here the under 14 boys jump up at the start of the sack race. The event was won by V. Reynolds with K. Templeton second and M. Cocks third.

Not to be outdone by the boys, the men lie down ready for the start of their race at the band sports day in 1908. The race was won by M. Brenton with G. Stannaway second and T. Cowl third.

As it was the band's sports day, it was only right that the bandsmen competed as well and this is the start of their 200 yard race which was won by R. Higgins. Another event on the day was the tug of war when the Town beat Peterville.

West Kitty Male Voice Choir, 1914. Back row, left to right: Simon Richards, Fred Wilcocks, Jack Richards, Charles Richards, Fred Harper, -?-, -?-, Will Pope, -?-. Middle row: John Osborne, Arthur Simmons, George Richards, Bert Harper, Edwin Richards, Percy Rogers, -?-, -?-, -?-. Front row: ? Harper, Harry Epplette, Sammy Mitchell, the Conductor, Capt. Prisk, Alfred Solomon, -?-, -?-, Joe Chenoweth.

A group of happy smiling faces on St Agnes beach, Whit Monday 1909. The event is not known but could possibly be a church outing. Everyone sits or stands on a bank of sand that was at the top of the beach (see picture top of p. 40) where the changing huts are today. The little girl in the front, fifth from the left, is Honnor Sawle with her sister Molly in the large hat behind her.

Six

The Railway

THE BEACON, ST AGNES

The railway between Chacewater and Newquay was constructed under the 'Great Western Railway (Truro to Newquay Railway Act) 1897'. The Act provided that the railway had to be constructed within five years from the passing of the Act. The line between Chacewater (Blackwater Junction) and Perranporth was opened for passenger traffic on 6 July 1903 and between Perranporth and Newquay (Tolcarne Junction) on the 2 January 1905. The railway lasted until 1963 when it closed; the last train running on the 4 February 1963. Above, a train leaves St Agnes Station heading towards Mount Hawke in 1905. A familiar sight for those entering St Agnes via the Seven Mile Stone Road during the first half of this century.

The building of the railway bridge over the road at the West End of Blackwater around 1902. Here we see the large number of men needed to build such a bridge and the tools they hold suggest their various trades – masons, carpenters and labourers.

From Blackwater the line continued towards Mount Hawke. Here the bridge at O Miles 44 Chains is being built. The bridge is on the road from Skinners Bottom to Blackwater where the entrance to 'Wheal Briton Coaches' is today. The structure appears to be made of concrete, unlike the cut stone used on the Blackwater Bridge. The wooden templates to form the arch are on the left against the embankment.

St Agnes Station under construction c. 1902. The contractor's temporary track has been laid to transport building materials and goes under the bridge being built on the Penwinnick to Goonbell Road.

The building of Wheal Liberty Viaduct between Goonbell and Mithian in 1902 by the contractor Mr Arthur Carkeek of Redruth. The viaduct has five arches each of 55 ft span. The piers are built of local stone and the arches formed of specially moulded blocks of concrete.

This photograph of St Agnes Station and the one below are two rare views that appeared in the *Railway Magazine* early in 1903, just before the opening of the line from Chacewater to Perranporth. A contractor's train pulls into a spotless new station. The fittings still have to be put into the lamp on the left.

The Goonbell side of the railway bridge on the Presingoll to Goonbell road looking towards St Agnes Station c. 1903. The photograph presumably taken to show the bridge. The two postcards on this page have 'Kodak' postcard printed on the back as does the view of Blackwater Bridge on p. 50.

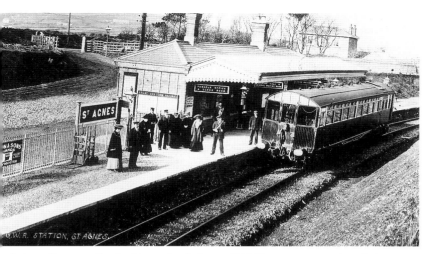

St Agnes Station staff and public on the platform c. 1905. The station, situated a mile from St Agnes village, did not please everyone and many used Goonbell Halt in preference.

Another view of St Agnes Station taken the same day as above. The station's platform looked like this until 1937 when an island platform was built making a passing point for trains on the stretch of line between Chacewater and Perranporth. The platform shown in the photograph was taken away and the canopy put on the other side of the building.

Mithian Halt c. 1930. A typical branch line halt with a pagoda shelter and oil lamps either side. In 1963 when the last train stopped at the halt, on route to Newquay, the guard Mr Boins turned out the solitary oil lamp, as was the custom every Saturday night but this time he brought it into the train. The second lamp had been stolen a week earlier!

Perranporth Station c. 1905 showing trains either side of the large island platform built in anticipation of a large tourist trade. When the last train in 1963 reached Perranporth, there was a television camera there to capture the scene as passengers, huddled in the cold, sang Auld Lang Syne.

Seven

Mining

For many centuries the area around St Agnes was noted for its tin mining. There is a well known Cornish saying 'Sten San Agnes an gwella sten in Kernow.' – 'St Agnes tin is the best tin in Cornwall.' Originally, the tin was worked by men burrowing into the cliff and hills without machinery. These workings are now called 'Old men's workings'. Later with the introduction of the steam engine, mines could be worked deeper and more profitably. Above, a group of miners pose outside Thomas' engine house. The man with the beard on the left is James Langdon, whose job it was to send the men up and down the mine shaft in the cage. He was very strict on time, and if a miner was only two minutes late they had to go down the shaft via the ladders.

West Kitty Mine c. 1895, showing on the left Reynold's pumping engine house and on the right the whim engine house. The mine worked from around 1863 to 1916, producing tin and a small amount of copper. The ore from the mine was carried by horse and cart to the stamps at Jericho Valley for dressing where the ore was crushed and the tin extracted. The mine was behind the main street in St Agnes. This view was taken from Trevaunance Road.

Thomas' Shaft of West Kitty mine c. 1905. The engine house contained a 40 inch pumping engine. The engine survives today in a dismantled state at the Science Museum in London. The man in the foreground is Charlie Uren riding a donkey shay, a very common form of transport at this time, mainly used by miners who travelled daily many miles to work. The engine house remains today at the rear of the pottery in Vicarage Road.

Wheal Friendly mine on the west side of Quay Valley c. 1908. Mine waste, today covered in vegetation, spills down the valley side. Wheal Friendly was taken over by West Kitty in 1900 and in 1907 pneumatic stamps and dressing equipment were installed with limited success, not least because of local objections to the calcining (burning) of the tin. They then reverted to the old Jericho Valley dressing floors which were updated.

Close up of Wheal Friendly mine c. 1905. This mine was abandoned during the First World War because of financial and manpower difficulties. In 1926 when Sarah shaft of Wheal Kitty mine was reopened to rediscover the great Wheal Kitty lode, Wheal Friendly was opened to ventilate the mine. The tunnels from both mines met up under Quay Valley. When Wheal Kitty closed in 1930, Wheal Friendly closed, never to start again.

Left: Wheal Friendly incline c. 1908 showing the rails from the mine down the valley side to Quay Road. The ore was taken from here by horse and cart through Peterville to Jericho stamps. As the full truck came down the incline, the empty one was pulled to the top. The building at the bottom of the hill is an old Wesleyan Meeting House, today a dwelling house called Fragments.

Below: Jericho Stamps c. 1908, situated in the valley between Barkla Shop and Trevellas Porth. All the ore mined under St Agnes village was brought here for dressing. At first the plant was powered by water wheels but later a steam engine, (in the centre of the view) was used.

TIN STREAMS, JERICO, Nr MITHIAN.

Blue Hills mine, Trevellas c. 1890. In the centre of the view is the 70 inch cylinder pumping engine and slightly to the left the large fly wheel of the horizontal engine which drove the stamps and did the winding for several shafts in the vicinity.

A J.C. Burrows photograph taken c. 1890 showing men working underground at Blue Hills mine at the 66 fathom level. The tin lodes here are 4 or 5 ft wide and very flat. Here men are putting in wooden pit props to support the hanging walls of killas. J.C. Burrows was one of the first photographers to use flash photography underground.

Left: In September 1906 a new mining company calling itself the Wheal Kitty and Penhalls United Limited was formed to work the Wheal Kitty area. At its half yearly meeting of mine shareholders on 13 August 1907, Mr J.H. Collins, the general manager, informed the meeting that the main work, since the company took possession, was at Sarah shaft, where the lofty staging and headgear had been erected to connect the shaft with the stamps. The men here are preparing to haul the staging into place above Sarah shaft using large chains and pulleys. This photograph and the next two were taken by the local photographer Sammy Solway, mentioned in the introduction, who worked at the mine.

Below: The wooden staging above Sarah shaft has now been completed and the building to the left contains the winding engine. The new pumping engine house is being built on the right to hold a 65 inch engine. The old 50 inch engine at the engine shaft, further inland, was unable to pump the water out of the depth of the mine sufficiently. The 'bob' that was to pivot on the bob wall above the shaft is being put into the engine house through the cylinder opening on the right.

Right: The bob being hauled onto the bob wall at Sarah shaft c. 1910. Each end of the bob was called a nose. The end connected to the main pumping rod was the outside nose and the end inside the house connected to the engine was the inside nose. The bob weighed many tons and it took precise manoeuvring to get the bob resting on the wall.

Below: Wheal Kitty mine c. 1926. Because of financial and manpower difficulties of the First World War, Wheal Kitty had to suspend operations in 1918 but the mine remained intact on a care and maintenance basis. In 1926 a new company was formed and the mine reopened with a new processing plant. Things started well with a rich lode being found. In 1930, however, there was a world wide slump in the price of tin and the mine was forced to close.

Another lovely Sammy Solway photograph showing the removal of the boiler from the engine shaft of Wheal Kitty mine c. 1912. After the building of the pumping engine at Sarah shaft this engine house had no use. The engine in it was built at Copperhouse Foundry, Hayle in 1852 for this mine. The engine was sold and taken to Parkandillick Clay works where it stands today. Here a team of at least nine horses is being used to take the boiler away from the engine house, seen behind in the distance.

On the 4 June 1905 there was a fire at the engine house for the stamps at Wheal Kitty mine. The fire was believed to have been started deliberately by a sacked employee. Only the bob wall remains with the huge bob on it. The postcard was sent to Grass Valley, California and the writer states, 'the man in the white jacket is Lobb Richards the engine man, then a stranger, then Whitford, then Jack Trezise, then Boosh Reynolds, John Donovan, boy Borlase on the wheel with Arthur Jones. Wheal Prudence is in the Background on St Georges Common!'

The re-building of the engine house c. 1905. To save the difficulties of taking the bob down it was supported in place and the engine house built around it. The outside nose of the bob was connected to the two large wheels causing them to revolve and in turn the wheels operated the stamps that crushed the ore.

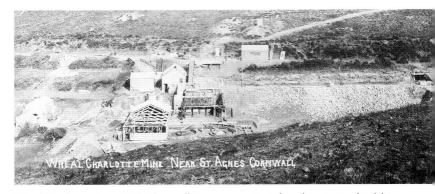

Wheal Charlotte mine c. 1912. This small tin mine was situated on the eastern side of the Chapel Porth valley, not to be confused with Great Wheal Charlotte on the cliff above Chapel Porth on the Porthtowan side. The mine worked by means of an adit level driven into the hillside, seen on the far right of the picture, and also from an inclined shaft further up the hill.

Mr Govier, who took the top picture, has now got all the staff to pose for him c. 1912 and it shows clearly the workings of a small mine. Once the ore had been removed from the hillside, it was stamped using the water wheel driven stamps, in the top of the view. Once the ore had been stamped to a dust, it was put onto the round buddle at the bottom where the tin was separated from the waste. The man in the bottom left hand corner is holding a miners vanning shovel.

New Wheal Leisure mine c. 1907 also known as Wheal Alfred was situated three quarters of a mile from Perranporth near the old Methodist chapel at Bolingey. The offices for the mine were in the cottage next to Bolingey Inn, shown in the photograph at the bottom of p. 75.

New Wheal Leisure mine opened in 1907 and worked until 1911 producing mainly zinc and a little copper and lead ore.

Left: Wheal Golden c. 1900 situated on the cliff 1¾ miles WNW of Cubert. The engine house was made of greenish/black clay slate and had a bright red brick castellated stack. The mine was active in the eighteenth century but the only record of output is for 1849-55 when 2,560 tons of 68 percent lead ore and 24,200 oz of silver were produced. During the Second World War the area comprising Wheal Golden and Penhale was taken over for the building of Penhale army camp. This resulted in the demolition of all engine houses including Wheal Golden and Penhale mine (below).

Below: The disused whim engine house of Penhale mine c. 1905. The mine was situated a short distance to the north of Perranporth beach. When working the mine produced copper ore and later silver and lead ore.

Eight

Churches and Chapels, Tea Treats and Outings

The small area covered in this book probably had as many churches and chapels as any similar size area in the rest of Cornwall. A high population during the mining boom of the nineteenth century meant the numerous churches and chapels were well supported with full congregations at every service. Every summer the tea treats were the high point of the year and people came from miles around to listen to the band and enjoy the tea and games. Above is the St Agnes Wesleyan Sunday School tea 1914.

Vicarage Road, St Agnes on Saturday 17 July 1909 and the Wesleyan Sunday School tea treat. Large numbers of old and present scholars joined in the procession as it was part of the centenary celebrations, the school having started in 1809. On the right are the remains of Fred James' butchers shop destroyed by the fire mentioned on p. 11.

The 1909, St Agnes Wesleyan tea treat at Churchtown. Music during the procession was provided by St Agnes Town Band and Truro Territorial Band. After the procession scholars under 18 were given a free tea and officers, teachers and scholars were each presented with a medal which was specially struck for the occasion.

St Agnes Wesleyan choir at Chapel Porth Friday 8 July 1910. Mr John Angwin the choirmaster is in the second row in the centre of the group. The choir are outside Mrs Tremewan's tea house that was situated on the cliff above the stream. She treated them to tea with strawberries and cream.

St Agnes Wesleyan tea treat at Peterville on Saturday 16 July 1910. St Agnes and St Dennis bands played during the procession around the village and at the tea afterwards. Unfortunately wet weather spoilt the day.

Maypole dancers at the St Agnes Wesleyan Sunday School tea on Saturday 15 July 1911. Many events took place including singing, reciting competitions and sports. Illogan Band under the Reverend Oxland was a major attraction.

Saturday 18 July 1914 and St Agnes Wesleyan Sunday School tea procession at the top of Town Hill. The procession numbers were less than usual and counter attractions drew the children away from the field and games. Note the shop on the top of Town Hill where the seats are today. There were two lock up shops here. No. 1 shown in the picture was a newsagent and stationer run by Miss Mary Sloggett. The second, adjoining, was a cobblers run by Joseph Quick.

Goonown Wesleyan Sunday School tea 16 July 1904, the procession having reached Peterville. In January 1904 Sir Edwin Durning Lawrence MP had given the chapel a donation of two guineas towards the renovation of their Sunday School.

Goonown Wesleyan Sunday School in 1904 hold their tea in the field near Goonown chapel. A great occasion with the fair with a merry-go-round and swingboats to help entertain the children and adults.

St Agnes Band of Hope tea at Churchtown on Monday 16 May 1910. The Band of Hope was founded in 1847 by Jabez Tunnicliff for all children under 16 years based on a simple pledge, 'I do agree that I will not use intoxicating liquor as beverages.' Some societies even mentioned tobacco, snuff and opium. Many societies started within existing Sunday Schools. Many children lapsed their pledge on reaching maturity.

St Agnes Band of Hope tea 1913. This picture has particular significance to the author of this book. The tall boy with the cap and glasses at the front right, is Percy Benney, the author's grandfather and the policeman in the top centre is Richard Henry Benney, Percy's father and the author's great grandfather! He was the village policeman from 1896 to 1919. He was also a local Methodist preacher and superintendent of the Sunday School.

New Connexion tea, St Agnes 1910. John Wesley expressed the desire that the Methodists should remain part of the Church of England. Some Methodists did not agree, one was Alexander Kilham who thought the Methodists should throw off their shackles with the Church of England. In 1791 he was expelled from the movement and together with other Methodist preachers formed the New Itinerency later known as the New Connexion.

New Connexion tea, St Agnes 1907 in a field close to the chapel at Rosemundy. The chapel in the top left of the picture, now the Masonic Hall, was built in 1835.

Mingoose Wesleyan Sunday School tea in July 1913. The Hungarian band provided the music during the tea, after which they had their fill of cakes, splits and tea. Their work however was still not finished, as at the end of the day they led the Serpentine Walk.

Beacon tea at Higher Bal in 1911. Having had their tea the children waited for the games with names such as 'Duff in the Back', 'Two's and Three's' and 'Kissing Ring'. Unfortunately rain during the afternoon spoilt some of the fun.

Above: The stone laying ceremony for the new Mawla Wesleyan chapel on the 8 July 1908. The new chapel replaced the old one that stood on the opposite side of the road to where the Sunday School building is today.

Right: People leave the opening ceremony of the new Mawla chapel. Mawla was the site of an ancient chapel that was situated by the side of the road to Menagissey about half a mile out of Mawla. In 1847 in a paper to the Royal Institution of Cornwall it was described as, 'recently occupied or used as a cowhouse. This building at Mawla as seen now is 25-30 feet long by 16 feet wide.' There is no sign of the chapel now but its location appears on early ordinance survey maps.

Mount Hawke Methodist chapel c. 1900. Situated in the centre of the village and bears the date 1820. It was built on a piece of land obtained from the Manor of Tywarnhayle for £2 plus 2 pence a year rental. Of the thirteen original trustees in 1820, eleven were miners, one a blacksmith and another a yeoman.

The band play in the road outside Mount Hawke Wesleyan chapel at their Sunday School tea c. 1908. After the procession from Banns to Short Cross and back, the tea and games were usually held in the field on the opposite side of the road to the chapel.

Skinners Bottom Methodist Sunday School tea c. 1908. Scholars and teachers prepare for their procession around the village. From the chapel they marched down the hill towards Mount Hawke where the band played at the end of the road. They then turned left to Ivy Chimney where the band played on the triangle of grass, now gone. From here they marched back to Skinners Bottom for the tea treat.

Skinners Bottom Sunday School tea treat 1911, held in Mr Rowe's field. Leaders of the Sunday School at this time were Will and Eddy Rowe. The Sunday School was established in 1869.

At 12 noon on Wednesday 15 March 1905 St Agnes church tower was struck by lightening. The steeplejack Mr Larkins of Bow, London was called in to examine the damage. He stated that the blow must have been of such a tremendous force that there was not a sound joint in the bottom of the steeple. It surprised him that the whole spire had not fallen. The steeple had to be taken down to the tower and totally rebuilt.

St Agnes band under their new bandmaster Mr Harry Robins, leads St Agnes church tea at Churchtown, Friday 28 July 1911.

St Agnes church Sunday School tea 1911. Everyone beautifully dressed with all the girls in white dresses and hats. Following the procession, tea and games were held in the field of Castle House. Unfortunately rain in the evening spoilt the enjoyment.

Cross Coombe Primitive Methodist chapel c. 1914. The Primitive Methodist Society was formed in 1811. A society at Cross Coombe first appears in 1835 and the chapel was built the following year. It was built to seat 210 people with choir seats behind the rostrum. At the back of the chapel the seats rose sharply and there was a classroom underneath. The chapel remained until the Second World War when it was demolished to extend the airfield at Trevellas.

Cross Coombe Primitive Methodist Choir c. 1906, in the choir seats behind the rostrum. Music for this was provided by an harmonium but later a pipe organ was installed. Members of the choir are: Back row, left to right: Sammy Aver, Austin Harris, Tom Harris, Bessie Piper, Sam Mitchell, Frank Piper, Irwin Mitchell. Front row: Minnie May, -?-, -?-, Rose May, Maude Harper, Ada May, Martha Harris, -?-, Mildred Wills, Ada Mitchell, -?-.

Cross Coombe chapel choir outing to Penzance on Saturday 8 June 1907, picking up members on the road by Mithian School. The choir master Mr Richard Harris stands on the road. The group travelled by Jersey car to Redruth where they caught the 8.20 a.m. train to Penzance and had a meal at Jennings Restaurant. After a visit to Newlyn to see the fishing fleet unloading they caught the 6.20 p.m. train to Camborne. After staying here a short while they took a tram to Redruth and Jersey car home.

The following year on Saturday 8 August 1908 the choir went to Falmouth. No train ride this year – horses all the way! At Falmouth they visited various sights and took a steamboat trip. They started the journey back at 7.30 p.m. arriving back at Cross Coombe at 11 p.m.

Cross Coombe Sunday School tea treat procession on Saturday 13 July 1907 headed by the banner carriers, then the Bugle Brass Band. On leaving Cross Coombe chapel, the procession went down London Lane to Menadue's shop (bottom p. 70) where the band played and hymns were sung. From here through Trevellas to Lavender Cottage where they turned and retraced their steps back to Trevellas as seen in the view above. The tea treat was held in Mr Berryman's field and the weather was glorious all day and evening.

Cross Coombe Sunday School tea treat c. 1912. All the boys tucking into tea treat saffron buns the size of dinner plates. In the picture are: Rear right: Monty Mitchell. Front left: Gutherie Thomas. Front centre: Clifford Mitchell and to his left: Clar Andrew.

Trevellas Downs, Sunday School tea procession, c. 1909, heading back up the hill towards the chapel. The band leading the procession is St Agnes, with the distinctive bandsman Charlie Chegwin in the front row. Obviously a very hot day as the bandsman on the right has undone his tunic jacket. In the distance are the fields and meadows that were turned into Trevellas Airfield during the Second Word War.

Trevellas Downs Sunday School tea 1914. A typical tea treat; trestle tables covered in white table cloths and bench seats. Many pots of tea drunk and tea treat saffron buns consumed. Music for the procession and tea treat was provided by Summercourt Band.

Mithian chapel c. 1905. The right hand, white part of the building was the chapel and an older building than the dark left hand side, which was the Sunday School. It is not known when the chapel was built but there was a Methodist Society in Mithian as far back as 1839. In 1985 the chapel was sold and converted into two large dwelling houses.

St Agnes Band, leading the Mithian Band of Hope tea procession in 1914, stop playing as they go from the Rose-in-Vale up the hill towards Mithian village. The procession had gone from the chapel down to the Rose-in-Vale where the band played and the children had sweets. They then went up to the village for the tea and games.

Mithian Band Of Hope tea, headed by Camborne Band in Mithian village in 1907. Having walked up the hill from the Rose-in-Vale, they are preparing to march off again to the carriage drive of Mithian Farm to have their tea treat food and games.

A close up of Camborne Band at Mithian Band of Hope tea treat in 1907. At this time Camborne was the best band in the county and were paid to attend the tea treat. Hundreds of people came from far and near to listen to them play.

Mithian Band of Hope tea at the carriage drive of Mithian Farm in 1907. More children who have signed the pledge not to drink alcohol. How many of these kept the pledge in later life?

Mithian Band of Hope tea, 1913. Festivities over, the band head back to Mithian chapel. This year Mr Govier photographed the event taking over from Sammy Solway who had attended and photographed the previous six years.

Mithian Choir outing to Newquay in 1907, taken outside the Men's Institute in Mithian before the porch was added. Mr Harry Mitchell's Jersey car is being used for the trip. For many of the steeper hills on route the choir members would have got off and walked to the top as their weight was too great for the horses to pull.

Mithian Choir off to Falmouth for their outing in 1908. This time three horses are being used. The journey took about three and a half hours each way.

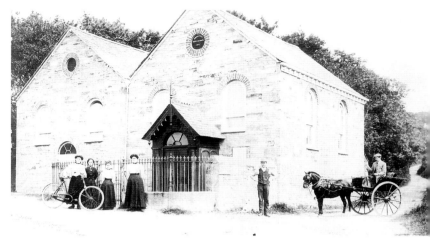

Perranwell Wesleyan chapel c. 1906. This chapel was built in two stages; the left hand side in 1843 and the right hand side in 1867, which is also when the small yard was added. In 1917 plans were drawn up to add another gable for a Sunday School but instead, in 1918, a wooden building was purchased from Nobel's factory at Cligga. The ladies beside the railings are believed to be Ellen Bown, the Pedlar Sisters and Jessie Varker. The chapel closed in 1986 through falling congregations and is now two dwellings.

The small Bible Christian chapel at Penhallow c. 1906, situated on the main Chiverton to Newquay road just before the Plume of Feathers public house. More recently the building has been used as a men's institute with a full size snooker table inside. The building looks very much the same today, except the windows near the road have been boarded up, presumably to stop vandalism.